# ANIMALS AT THE ZOO: FUN ANIMALS WE LOVE

**SPEEDY PUBLISHING**

Speedy Publishing LLC
40 E. Main St. #1156
Newark, DE 19711
www.speedypublishing.com

Copyright 2015

All Rights reserved. No part of this book may be reproduced or used in any way or form or by any means whether electronic or mechanical, this means that you cannot record or photocopy any material ideas or tips that are provided in this book

Zoos around the world are trying to coordinate efforts to breed endangered species.

The giraffe is is the tallest land animal in the world. Fully grown giraffes stand 5-6 meters tall. The males are taller than females.

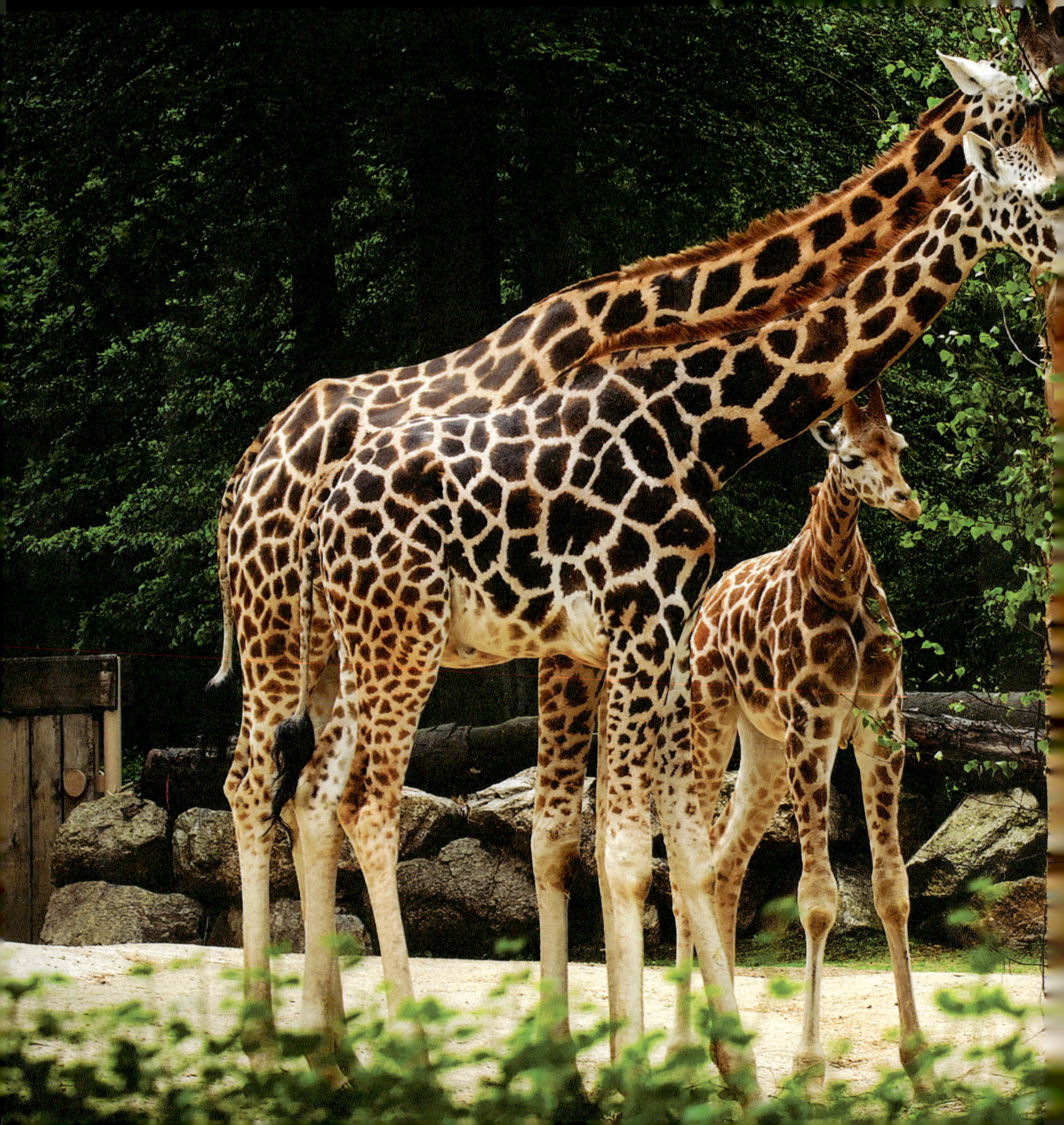

Giraffes use their height to browse on leaves and buds in treetops that few other animals can reach.

The koala is a tree-dwelling marsupial mammal. Koalas are native to Australia. They can only be found in the eucalyptus forests.

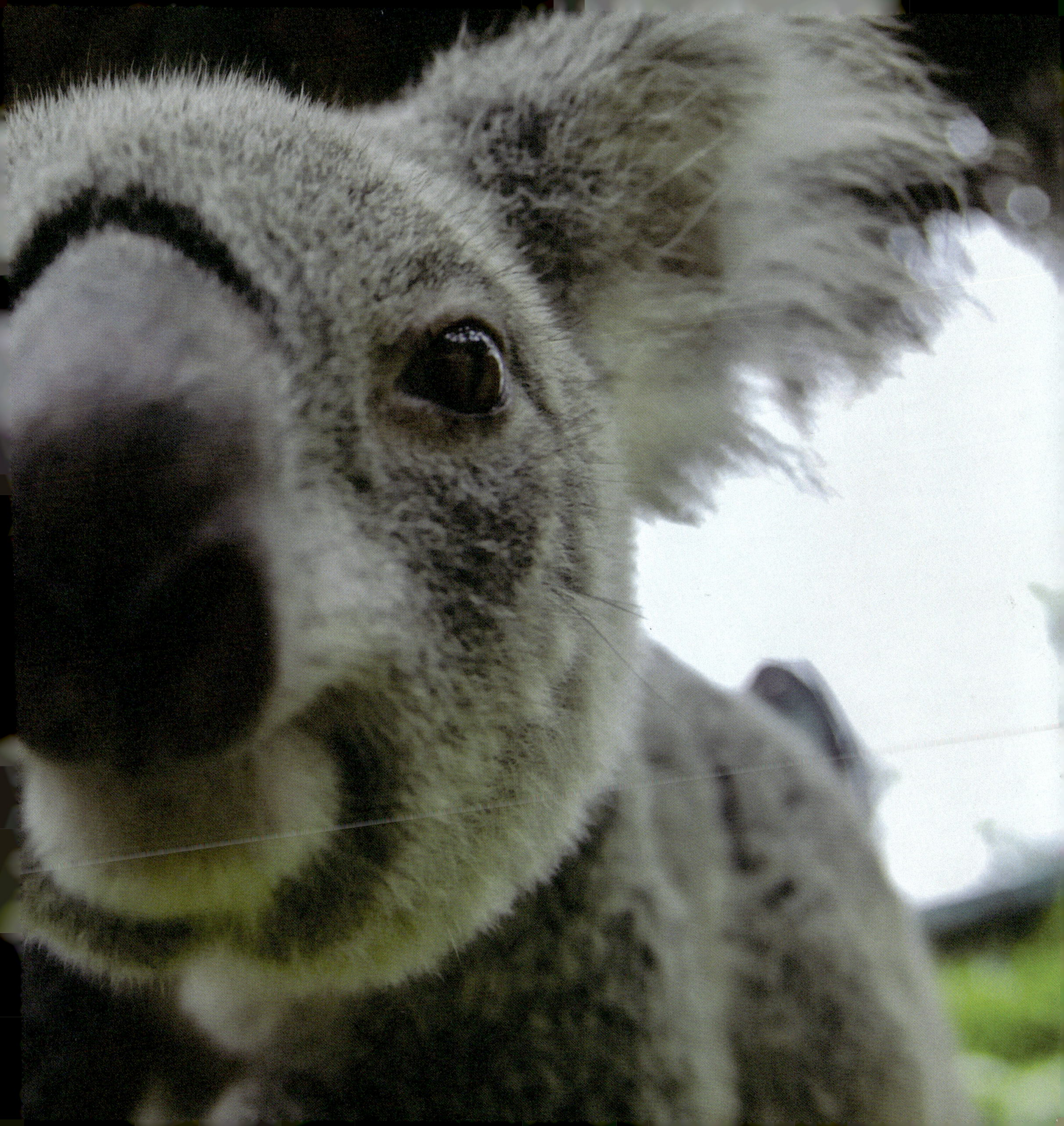

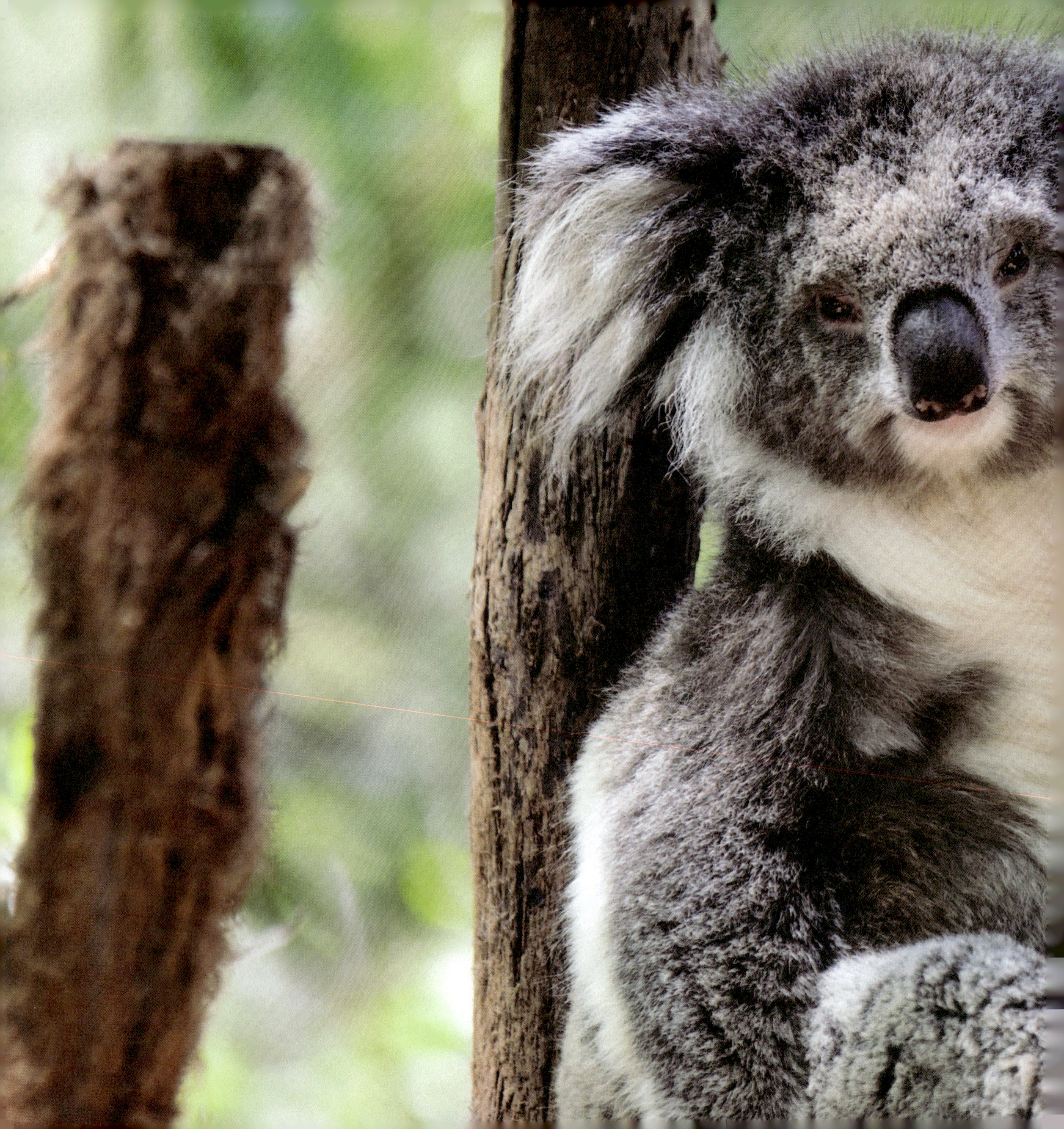

The word "koala" means "no drink" and it refers to their ability to go for many days without water.

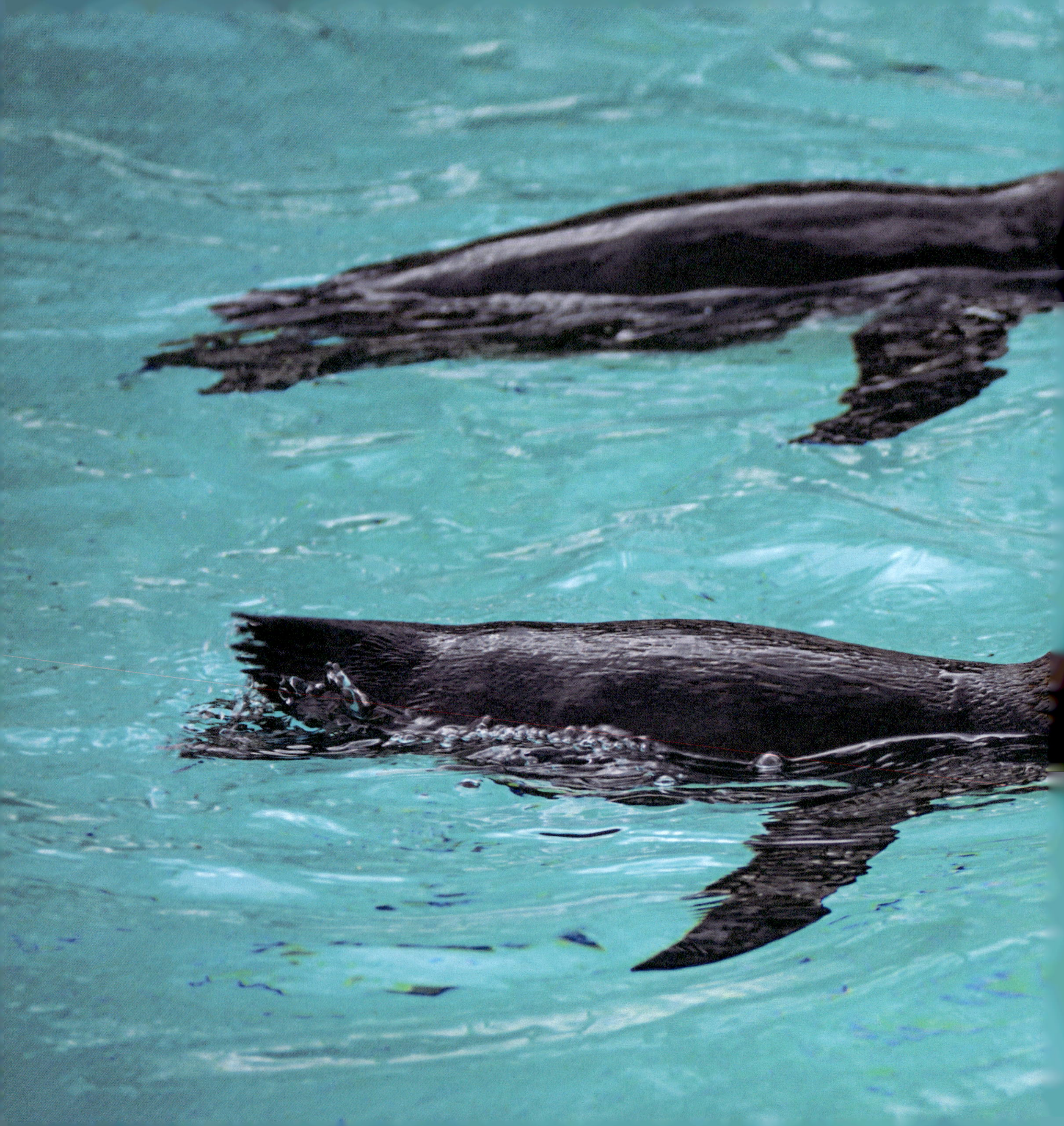

Penguins are a group of aquatic, flightless birds living in the Southern Hemisphere. Penguins have adapted flippers to help them swim in the water.

Penguins have excellent hearing and rely on distinct calls to identify their mates when returning to the crowded breeding grounds.

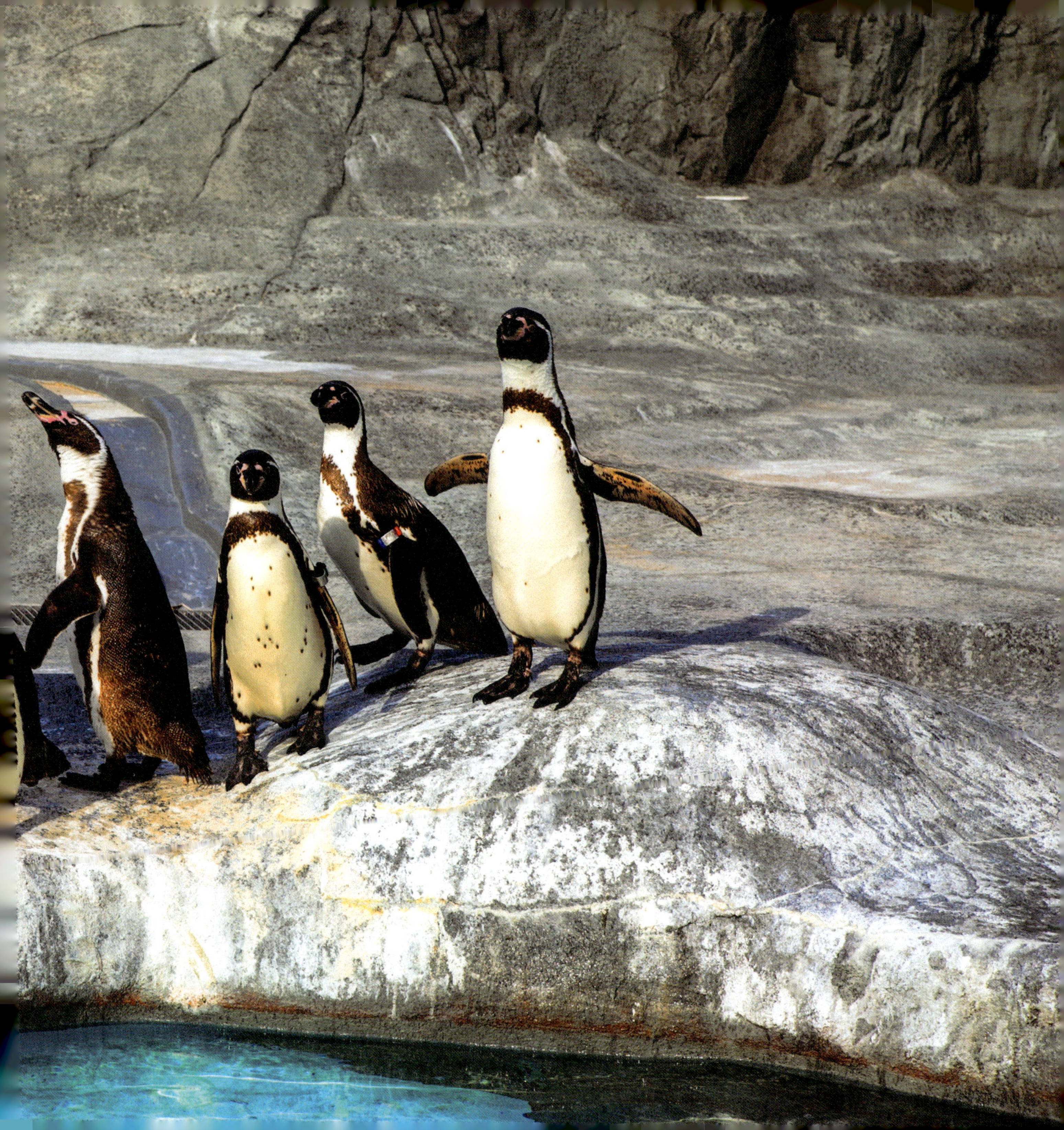

Peafowl belong to pheasant family. Male peafowl is called peacock while female is called peahen.

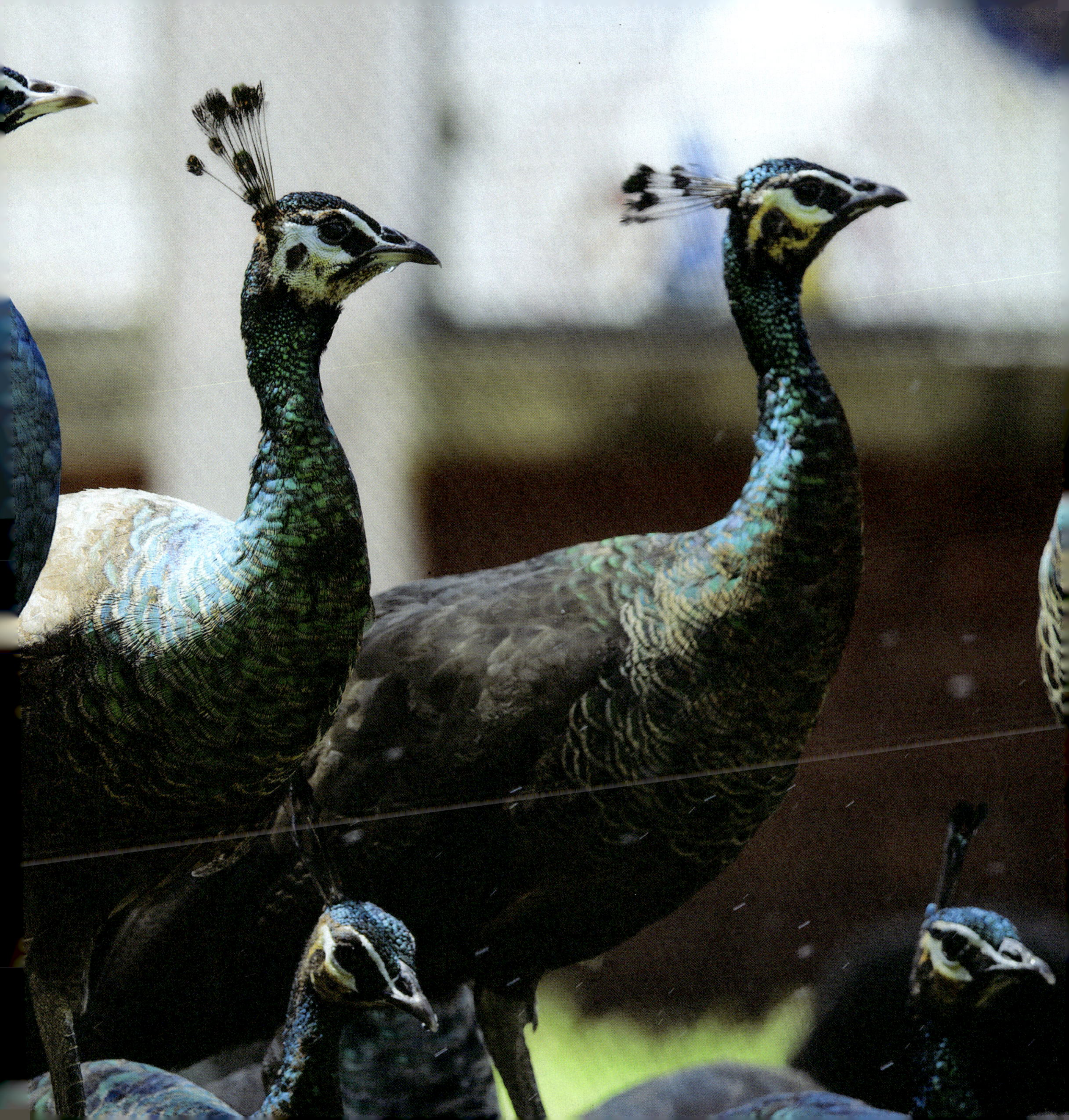

Peacocks are known for their amazing eye-spotted tail feathers. It is is believed to be a way to attract females for mating purposes.

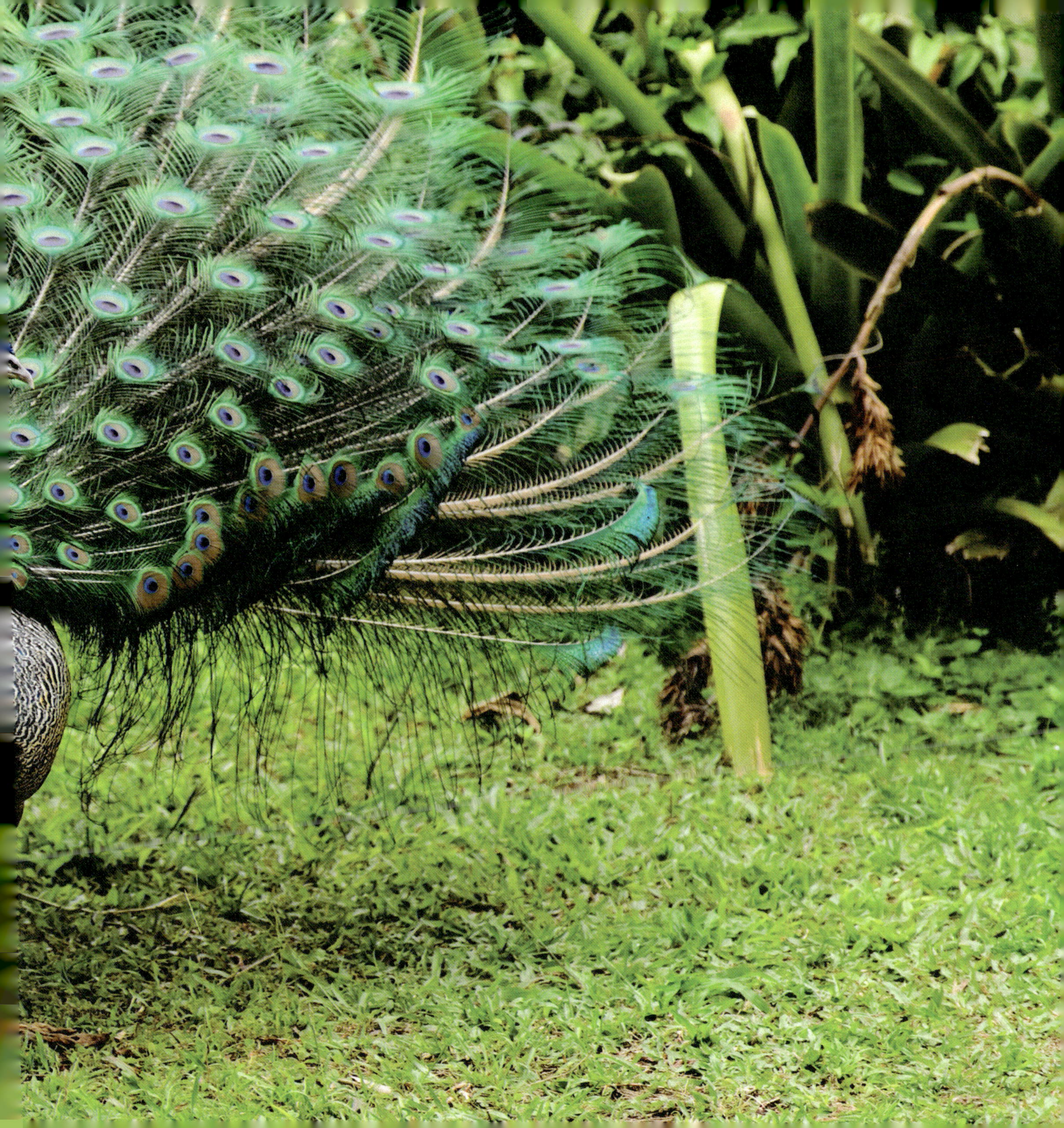

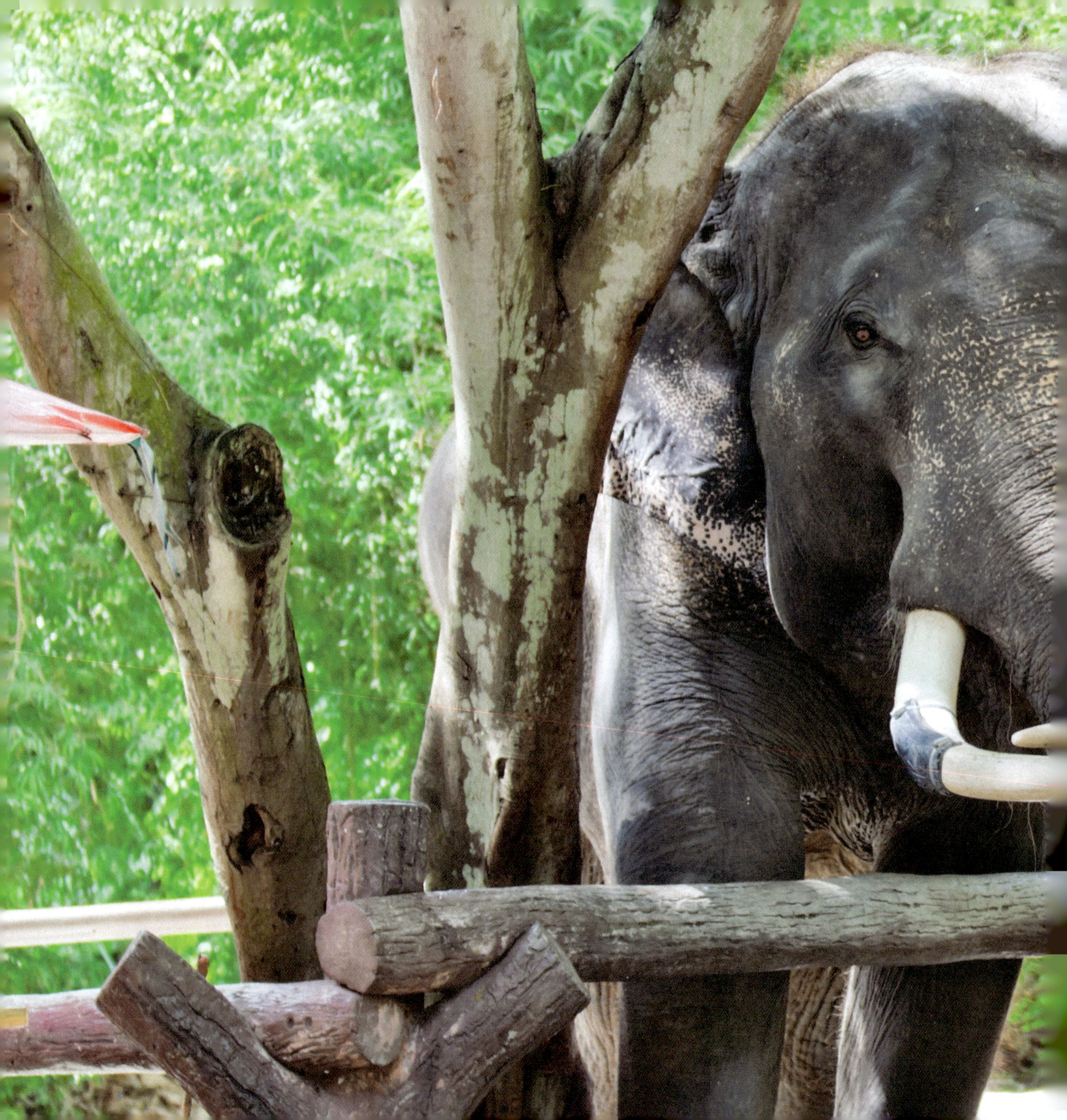

Elephants are the largest land-living mammal in the world. They live in Asia and Africa. Adult elephants weigh between 5,000 and 14,000 pounds.

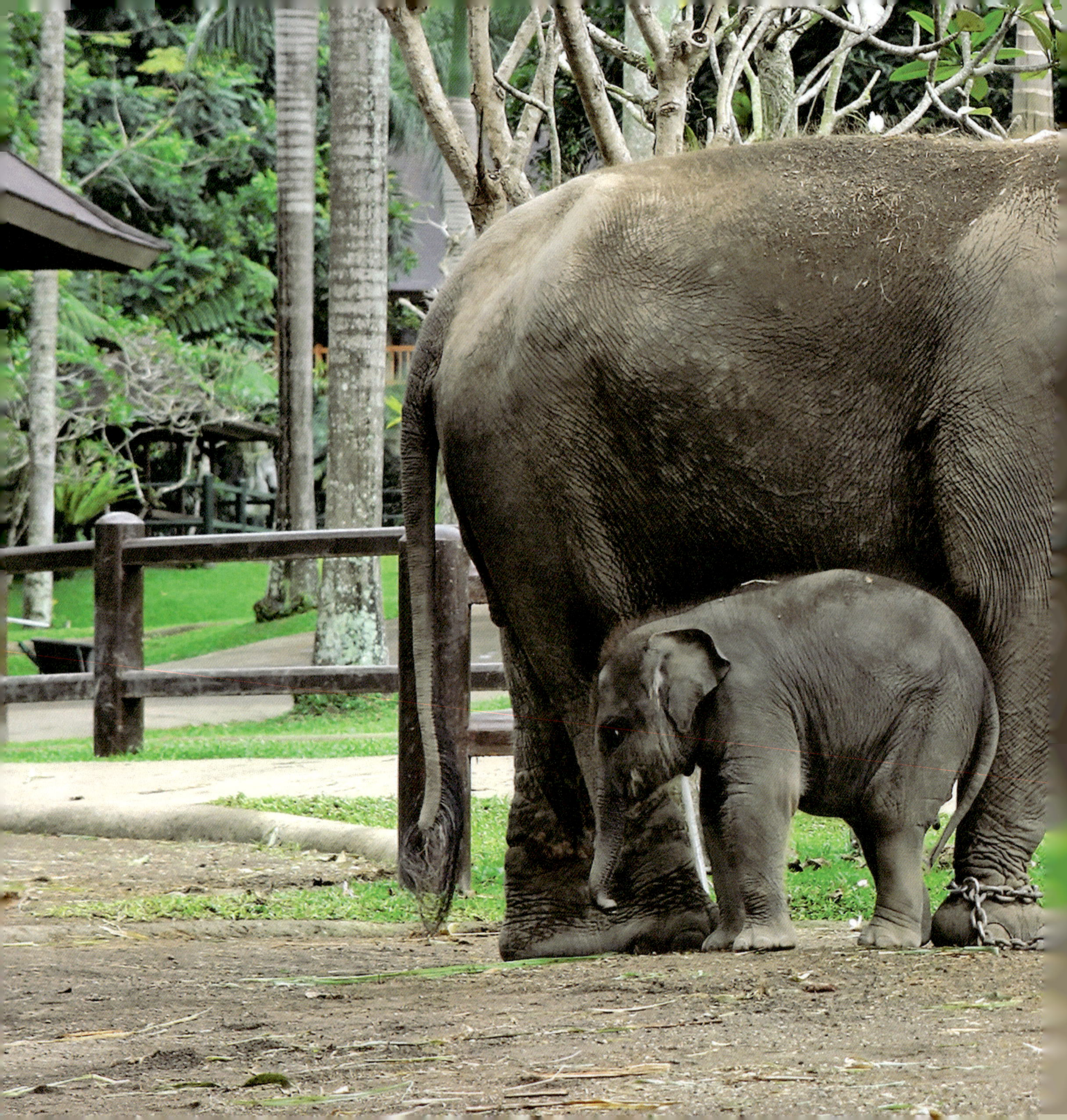

Elephants spend 16 hours a day eating. They eat grass, leaves, shrubs, branches and fruits.

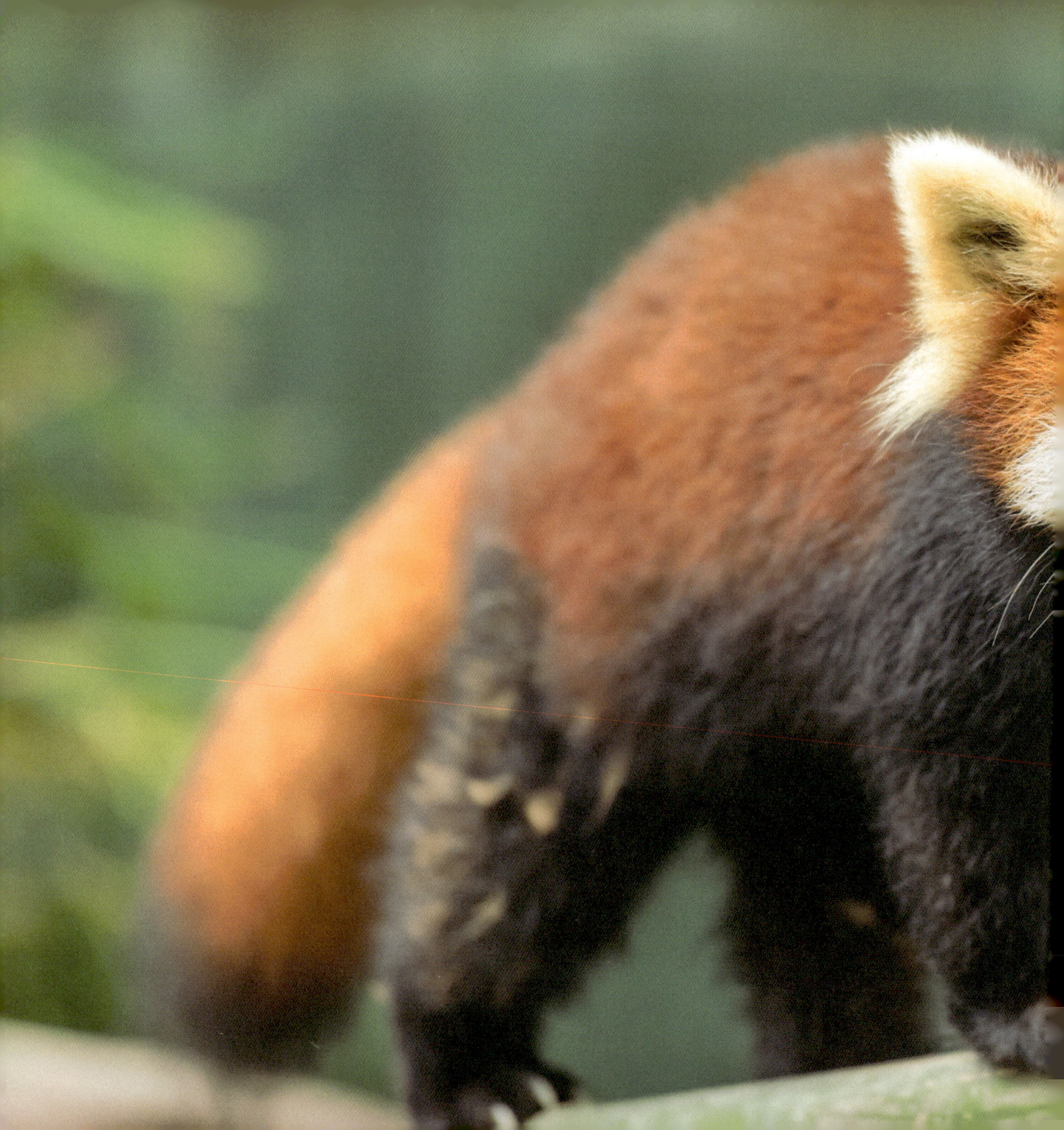

Red panda is a close relative of giant panda. They are also known as 'fire fox' because of its red color of the fur.

Red Pandas spend most of their time in trees. They live in Sichuan and Yunnan provinces of China, Himalayas, Myanmar and Nepal.

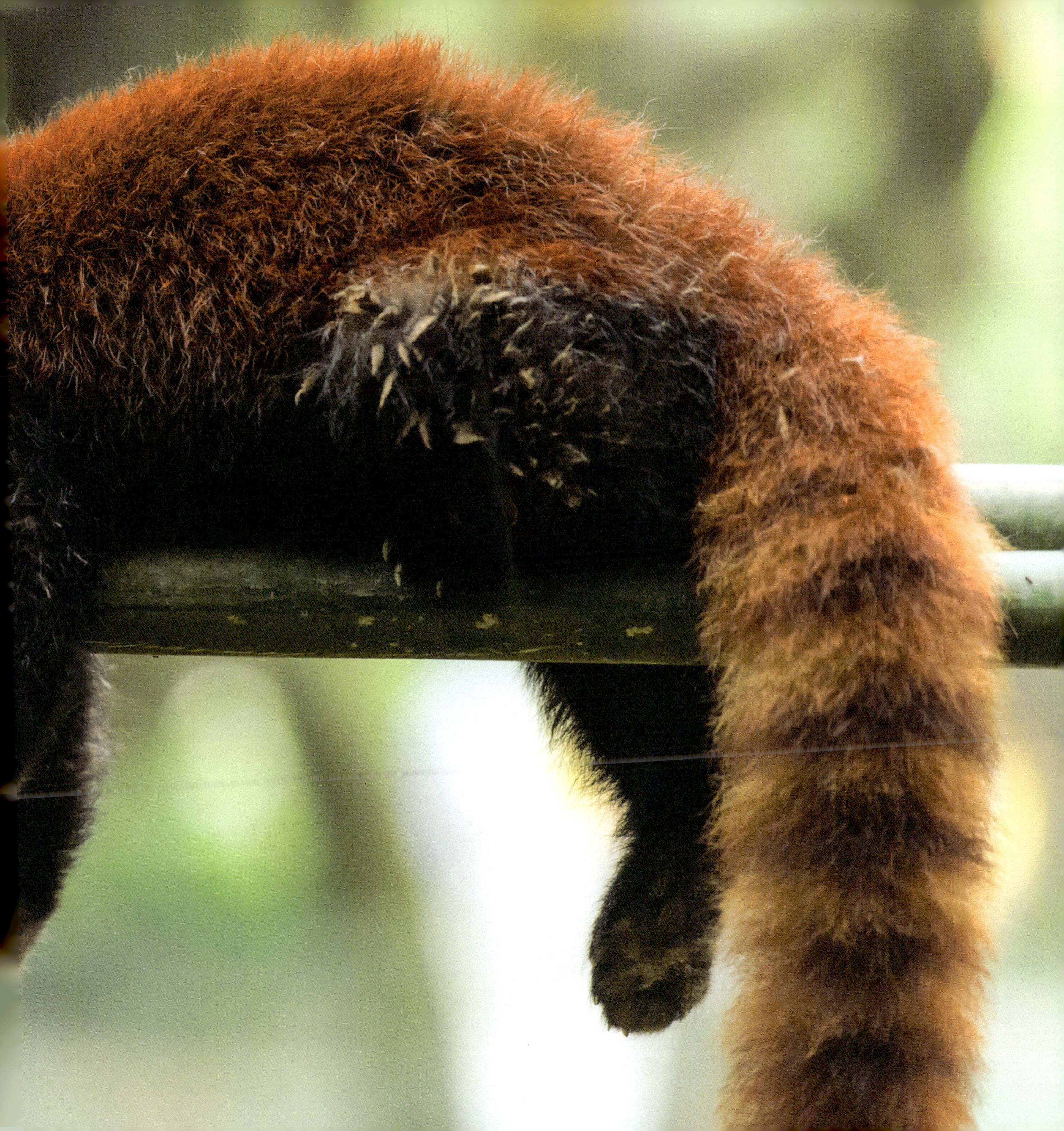

Zebras are members of the horse family. Every zebra has a unique pattern of black and white stripes.

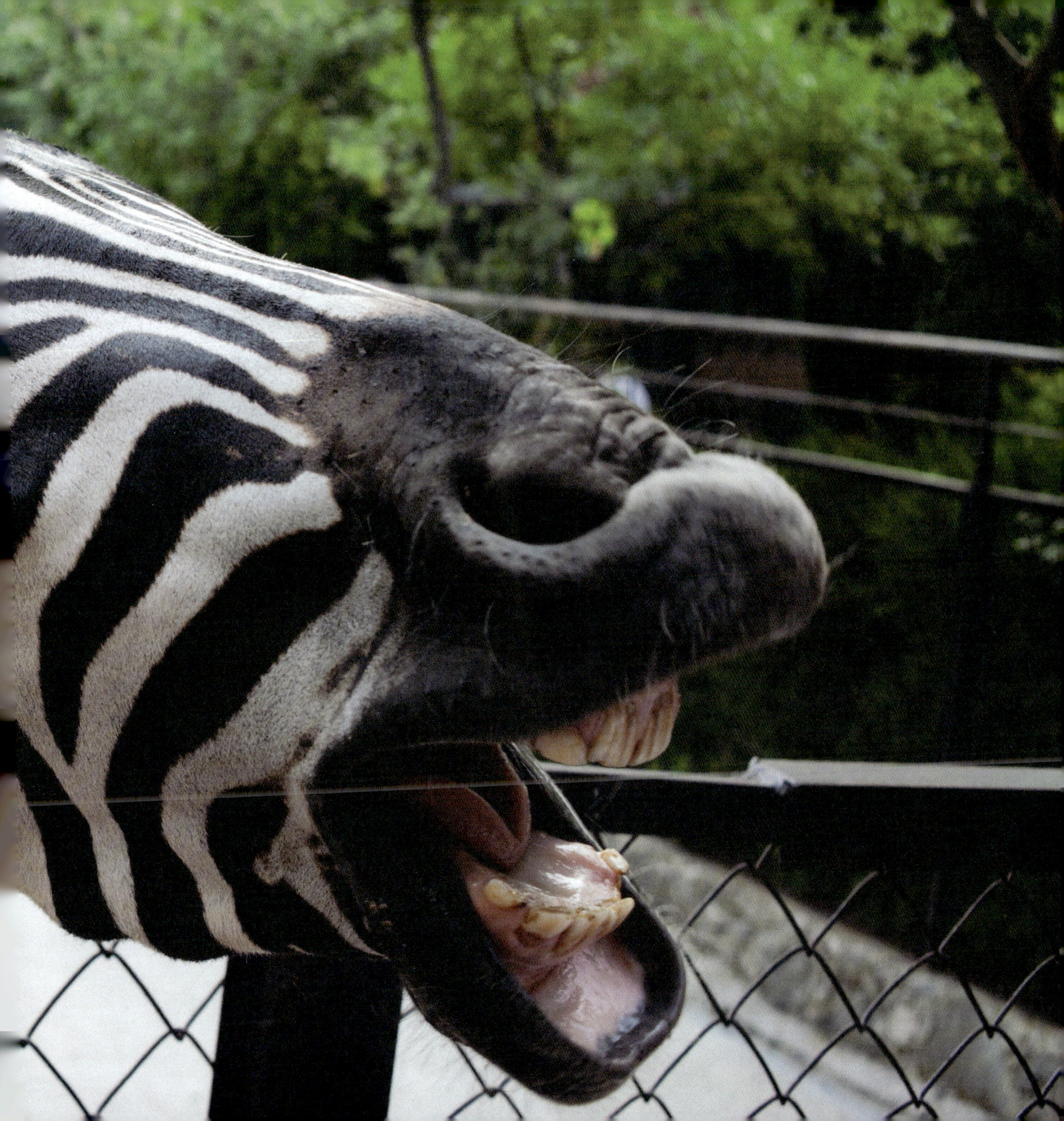

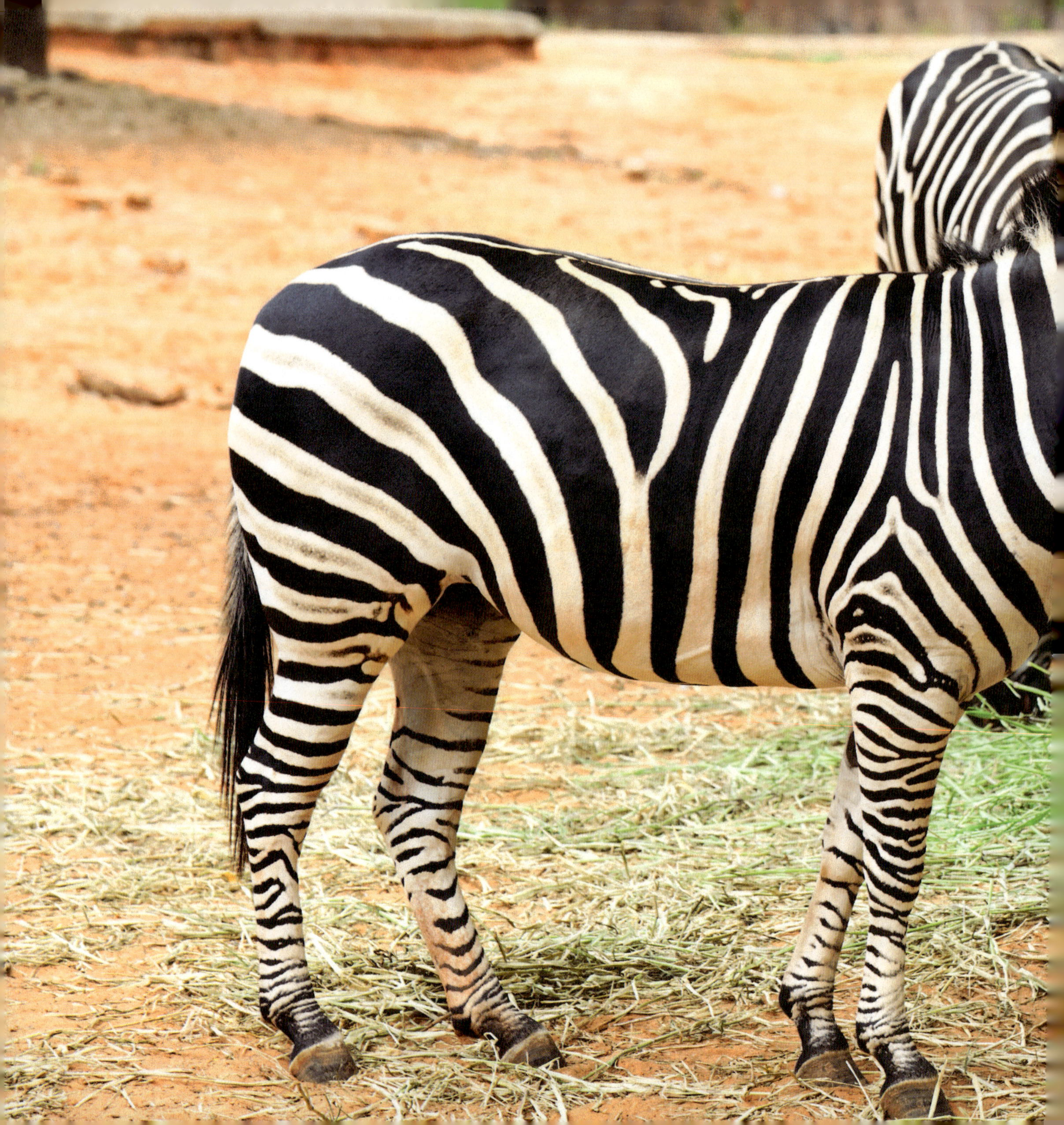

When a zebra is attacked other members of it's herd will form a circle and face the predator to help the attacked zebra.

Printed in Great Britain
by Amazon